MW01171306

# Mommy, Can I Change My Name?

## *Raising Children Across Cultures*

Bola Fenny, JD. PhD

Copyright © 2023

All Rights Reserved

*To my husband, Enefaa, who ensures the ship stays afloat.*

# Acknowledgments

*A big thank you to "Uncle" Ndaeyo Uko, Paul and Nosh Nwabuikwu, and Zika Nwunye Chikezie for reading and offering useful suggestions for the manuscript.*

# About the Author

Bola Fenny was raised in Ibadan, Nigeria. She got her bachelor's in law from the University of Benin, Nigeria, a Masters in criminal justice from the University of Alabama at Birmingham, and a Ph.D. in criminology from the University of Texas at Dallas. She was called to the Nigerian Bar in 1989 and admitted to the Alabama State Bar in 2010. She has been married to Enefaa Fenny for 29 years, and they have two adult children. She has been a Pastor's wife for 26 years and a practicing attorney for over 30 years. Bola and her husband relocated to the United States in 2002, and together they Pastor the Redeemed Christian Church of God Jesus House Birmingham. Bola is passionate about teaching and has been a college professor for over 10 years. She is the minister in charge of the children's ministry at Jesus House Birmingham. She hosts the cutting-edge YouTube channel, "Cross-culture with Bola".

# Table of Contents

# Preface

I am an empty nester, and my kids are doing pretty well. Many times, I wonder how I made it over. I wonder what it took God to get me to this point. Don't get me wrong, I am not there yet, and my kids are still a work in progress. But I have come a long way in this journey of parenting. I am not too sure how that should feel yet, but in this season of my life, younger parents look to me for advice assuming that I have done something right in my early parenting years. It is both amusing and humbling. Sometimes I wish they knew some of what it took to get "here", how often I failed my kids, and the regrets I have. My kids are okay (at least, I think so)! They didn't turn out badly at all, and there's so much to be thankful for.

My son is a practicing attorney, and my daughter is an Air Force Officer/law school student. That sounds pretty cool, right? But as they say, not all that glitters is gold. My children are my gold, but beneath the surface of these golds, there are scars. There were some painful years of sorrow, tears, and blood. I didn't always live up to expectation-God's and theirs-and it led to some very tumultuous years in our relationship. And while we are at a better place now, we are not "there" yet. We still butt heads-sometimes about little things and a few times about big things. We have irreconcilable differences, and hopefully, as the years go by (maybe when they become parents, they will have an appreciation of the challenges,) we will shout Kumbaya!

My kids were 6 and 2 years old, respectively, when we arrived in Atlanta on the 28th of February 2002, Enroute Birmingham, Alabama. My son started school on Monday, the 7th of March, and our home has not been the same since that "fateful" day. On the 19th of March, precisely 19 days after we arrived, it was our wedding anniversary, and my son's questions caught me unaware.

"How long have you been married?"

"8 years," came my quick reply. His response was as quick as my response,

"Wow, eight years and no divorce, good job." I froze.

"What's the meaning of divorce?"

Without missing a beat, he replied, "When married people are no longer in love, then they divorce."

I looked perplexed at him. "Who told you that?"

"Hmmm...you don't know? That means you don't know what I know."

That was my shocking introduction to cross-cultural parenting. In less than two weeks in school in the States, my six years old son had picked up on the concept of divorce. Though divorces occur in Nigeria, they are few and far between and typically discussed behind closed doors among adults. I sighed deeply, unsure that I had the required tools to navigate this new world.

Welcome to cross-cultural parenting!

It has been a turbulent ride. But God's grace has been abundant for each step. We have survived some very scary patches on this journey. We have been hit by some fiery bullets and stepped on some landmines, but thankfully, we made it "here". We made it through the dangerous patches, and we are still praising the Lord for seeing us through. Our story is not universal, but the principles enunciated in this book, mainly gleaned from the scriptures, have universal relevance. The God who saw us through and is still holding our hands is not limited by time, place, or circumstance. He is the same yesterday, today, and forever.

# Introduction

Parenting is probably the only life-long "occupation". As much as we promise to love and to hold until death do us part, marriages are not necessarily life-long. Divorce happens, and as much as we hate to admit it, it is more common today than God intends. However, we do not divorce our kids, and cases of Parent/Child estrangement are generally few. Kids leave our homes but never our hearts. They are irreplaceable. The bond is stronger than we can articulate. The job of parenting starts before the child is born. It starts with the realization that we are pregnant. We chose our meals, clothes, shoes, recreation, and everything based on the health and well-being of the baby. Everything changes once the baby arrives- sleeping patterns, expenses, outings, and even our relationship—all these changes we make very joyfully. The baby becomes the center of our world. But then life happens, and in this globalized world, we move from one culture to the other. Navigating a new culture is typically easier for children than for adults, and sometimes this process can create tensions in our family dynamic. If poorly managed, it could lead to fractured relationships. In the extreme, they could cause irreparable damage.

Cross-cultural parenting is nothing new. Living across your natural boundaries is natural and scriptural. In Genesis 12:1, God told Abraham to:

*"Get out of your country, from your family, and from your father's house to a land that I will show you".*

God meant business. Abram had to "get out" of his "country". He was not to move to the next county, city, or state. God's instruction was to leave his country. And just in case Abram misunderstood the command, God told him he was to leave his father's house. God did not mince words. He left no room for confusion. There had to be a break. A separation from everything Abram had ever known. God was requesting a total break from the known to the unknown. God did not give Abram the benefit of knowing where he was going. He could not set his GPS; he needed to hear and listen to God for his destination. I wonder how Abram conveyed this message to his wife. Sarai must have thought there was a loose nut in her husband's head. But they moved. At the Lord's command. Abram's story was unique because God specifically commanded him to move to an unknown destination (to the land that I will show you). For 21st-century parents, it is life. Circumstances, jobs, and differing situations move us from where we are, to a "strange land" where we must raise our kids. Whether the kids are born or brought to a foreign land, the challenges are the same. The kids are simultaneously exposed to two cultures—the parents' and the foreign lands. Navigating both cultures can be challenging. Most kids learn to "code-switch". They adapt to the culture of the new environment in public and assume their parents' culture at home. Code-switching is not as easy as it sounds. It can be stressful for the kids and cause conflicts with the parents. Few parents accept the foreign culture, some resist it, and resistance to the new culture inhibits parents' ability to connect with their children.

I should know. My parenting started back in Africa. Both my kids were born in Nigeria, where I had the whole village "on speed dial" as I learnt the ropes. I had people coach, help, support, and scold me as I faltered along. Comparatively, parenting was easier in Nigeria. My kids were always in good hands. All that changed when I came to the US. For the first year or two, it was my husband and I in the grind, trying to figure out parenting in this new culture. For a while, it was like we were flailing in the wind. It was a culture shock. My kids didn't have neighborhood friends and aunties like they did in Nigeria. The aunties and uncles that spoilt them endlessly were thousands of miles away. They were almost always indoors with the TV for company. My two-year-old especially didn't understand the change and kept asking for the aunties she had known in her short life. I do not recall her being satisfied with our answers, but I remember feeling sorry for taking her away from her comfort zone. Between our frequent trips to the library for the reading programs, regular attendance of a family-oriented church, and watching daily child-friendly PBS children's programs, she adjusted to her new environment. The adjustment didn't come easy for us. Our immigration paperwork, projected to take three months, took nine years. We could not work. Doing anything illegal was out of the question, so we lived by faith, literally speaking. We did without even the basics sometimes, but we made it. The fact that we did not have as much disposable income as we did in Nigeria made out situation even more stressful.

Psalm 137 is a rendition of the experiences of the Israelites when they lived as captives Babylon. Everything about Babylon was strange and rather than continue in the worship of Jehovah, they hung their instruments of worship and wept. The Babylonians knowing their proclivity for singing requested a song, but the Israelites wallowed in self-pity and could not sing. They hung on to memories of the good old days in Zion and refused to sing the Lord's song in a strange land. I am not sure why, but Boney M's rendition of this song in the 70's was an instant hit. The song made greater sense to me when I began my sojourn in a strange land.

I resisted and fought my kids' assimilation into this strange culture. In my naivety, I reasoned that my culture was superior. And in that mindset, I pushed my children to be Nigerian in all spaces without realizing they were better off understanding their spaces and adapting. I remember scolding my son whenever he would refer to our neighbor by his first name. In my culture, male adults are "uncles" or "broda", while female adults were "aunty". My neighbor ultimately set me straight. He would rather be Mike and not uncle. Those were rough and painful years. I didn't have people who were hands-on to show me how to raise culturally intelligent children, and my children suffered in the process. If I had a penny for the many mistakes, mis jives, and misdoings of those early years, Jeff Bezos would have nothing on me!

This book answers a few of the questions younger parents ask about thriving in a different culture. How to raise culturally intelligent kids? How to adapt to a new culture? Principles for retaining your identity in a new culture. This is not a know-all or the answer for all situations, but it contains some information that will help you navigate our cross-cultural world. Globalization has opened borders and ensured that most societies are diverse. People of diverse people groups, tongues, and proclivities, co-existing in spaces that used to be monolingual, monoethnic, monocultural, and monotheist. The challenge is to live peacefully despite our differences and to retain our identities in a multicultural context. To parent in accordance with our values despite the push and pulls of competing cultures/values. This book helps you walk that path of cultural adaptability without losing your identity. Hopefully, you will find the information helpful in navigating your specific circumstance. If that happens, then it will be worth the time and mission accomplished!

# Before the Rivers of Babylon

Nigeria is a beautiful country of 200 million black people, three major people groups, several hundred minority groups, 250 different languages, and two major religions with the African traditional religion and new age doctrines in the mix. That is the very definition of diversity. We share spaces, intermarry, and have a general appreciation of diversity. Most families are religious, and despite the cultural differences, a thread runs through-Respect for elders is huge. Children do not look their parents in the eye. It takes a village to raise a child, and the size of the village is constantly evolving. Honoring your parents is not restricted to biological parents but everyone who stands in the place of parents.

Some parents send their kids off to boarding schools away from home for high school education. It was the place where children from the cultures co-existed and thrived.

I grew up in a culture where parents showed but did not express love. Love was assumed and hardly verbalized. We were fed, clothed, housed, educated, and married off because our parents loved us. We were also paddled (probably abused) because our parents loved us. We didn't feel abused; though looking through today's lens, it would appear we were. Our parents' action was based on their limited knowledge. And considering how we all turned out, they did a good job. Our culture was communal. We were in each other's business, and we didn't mind.

I didn't know I was black. It was not because I didn't look in the mirror daily, but color was not an issue in Nigeria. We are all black people of different ethnicities. My blackness only became an identifier when I arrived in the United States. Nigerian parents pay for their kids' education for as long as they stay in school. Which in some cases means till they obtain their Ph.D. Children live at home until they get married, except if they get a job out of state, in which case they will probably stay with relatives. There is no talk of being an adult at 18. You do what you are told or sometimes use your initiative. Talking back at your parents is disrespectful, and children are to be seen and not heard. Parents raise their children to protect the family name and honor. Parenting is seen as a God-given assignment, and parents strive to make sure their kids turn out well. The mantra is "remember the child of whom you are," —meaning you represent the family in whatever space you occupy. Parenting is a serious business. It entails provision, protection, and support, and not to forget the generous use of the rod.

Gen 2: 15-17 introduces us to the man God created. God made the heavens and the earth and spent a couple of days making provisions on the earth. Then He created man. Verse 15 tells us of His provision for His children:

*"Then the LORD God took the man and put him in the garden of Eden to tend and keep it. And the LORD God commanded the man, saying, "Of every tree of the garden you may freely eat; but of the tree of the knowledge of good and evil you shall not eat, for in the day that you eat of it you shall surely die."*

God put this man in the garden He had created. He did not leave him to figure things out by himself. He made provisions for man to survive and thrive and put boundaries in place. God "put him in the garden", and made sure he was comfortable, but he had to work- "tend and keep" the garden and maintain the boundary God put in place: "but of the tree of the knowledge of good and evil you shall not eat".

God (the parent) gave specific instructions to the man (His son) He created. God came down in the cool of the evening for quality time with the man. They had meaningful and inspiring conversations. The son could enjoy his Father's presence, ask questions, and have company to go through life. God gave time to His creature. He was God enough to create man and loving enough to hang out with His son. The son did not just enjoy his Father's provision but also his Father's company. He knew what to do and not do. He knew what was important to Dad. God did not love His son too much to set boundaries. He showed him what fruit to eat and which to stay away from. He told His son what was good for him and what would poison their relationship. God was clear, concise, and intentional in the instructions to His son. His Father was rich, but he had to work to preserve what his Father had provided. He was taught responsibility. He had to preserve his Father's wealth for future generations.

It is instructive that although God came down in the cool of the evening to fellowship with His son, God knew His son needed more. He was not a selfish Father. He was willing to let His son enjoy life, even if it meant spending time with someone else. God anticipated His son's need. His son did not tell God he was alone or lonely. God was proactive. He saw His son's need and met it without being asked. What a good Father. God stepped aside when the woman came into the picture. He allowed them to figure things out. God gave specific instructions concerning Adam's relationship with Eve. Genesis 2:24 says:

> *"Therefore, a man shall leave his father and mother and be joined to his wife, and they shall become one flesh."*

Adam was to be one with his wife. They were to be one flesh, and God would see them as such. I dare say that God knew they would fall and made provision for a soft landing.

In Gen 1:28, God blessed and commanded man to:

*"Be fruitful and multiply; fill the earth and subdue it;
have dominion over the fish of the sea, over the
birds of the air, and over every living thing that
moves on the earth."*

The practical implication of this blessing is
parenthood. Psalm 128 says children are the Lord's
heritage. Children do not arrive with an owner's manual
or a to-do list. Our cultures, training, experiences, and
instincts take over when we have kids. We do a lot of stuff
and repeat whatever works.

God's expectation of us as parents is to follow His
example of provision for our children and anticipating
their needs. God brought man into an environment of
provision. His basic needs were met, and God spent time
with His son in the cool of the evening. We must never be
too busy to spend time with our children. Our children
must be attuned to our voice, value system, and
expectations. They must feel secure in our love. We must
set and explain boundaries in clear and concise terms.

There were consequences to disobedience "for in the
day that you eat of it you shall surely die". God not only

told him to stay away from the fruit of knowledge of good and evil, but He made him aware of the consequence of eating the fruit. God did not remove the fruit from the garden. He left it, and his son was free to stay away from it or disobey his Father. Before the kids came, Adam and Eve disobeyed, and God wielded the big stick. He loved them too much not to hold them accountable. He did what he said he was going to do. He sanctioned their misbehavior, but while sanctioning them, He provided a path to restore their broken relationship. God did not abandon his kids due to their misbehavior. He was still a dad despite their disobedience. He did not excuse, justify, or ignore their misbehavior. He drove them out of the garden but made provision for them on the outside. God put his purpose above his relationship. He did not let His purpose for the world suffer due to man's disobedience. He had things in perspective.

The average African parent strives to be "God" and this is "good" in parenting their children. We "command" our kids to follow a set of rules, and we want to wield the big stick when they disobey. This comes easy in the African context but becomes challenging in a new culture. The new culture frowns at, and even criminalizes the sanctions that we consider normal. The children pick up on this and begin to buck the system and our values. However, since the cushion the African environment provided is removed, things change, most times for good, but in a few cases for the worst.

# By the Rivers of Babylon

The children of Israel were taken captive to Babylon —a strange place populated by idol worshippers. Babylonians had no covenant with God, and they desecrated the Holy Temple of God in Jerusalem. The Israelites suffered the indignity of serving Babylonians who had no regard for their God. So, they sat by the rivers of Babylon pondering, reminiscing, and weeping. They remembered Zion, and they wept. Rivers of Babylon is that strange place where your culture collides with a strange culture. For the average African, the place of your sojourn may be — Europe, America, Asia, or elsewhere. Like they say, America is a leveler. So, you come in as a doctor, nurse, lawyer, or whatever your profession is, and your degree is not recognized "here". So, you must study to take exams for certifications because, like they say, your degree is not recognized "here". Standing by the shores of the Rivers of Babylon tries your patience: kids young enough to be your child call you by first name and give you instructions. It's very jarring, but after a while, you get used to it. Your kids come back from school and tell you, "Hi, Mom" and you wonder if they drank "something". You proceed to do what the African parents do best (whooping), and the child says, "Mommy, my teacher says if you beat me, I should call 911". 911? What's that? You are immediately schooled that what we know as a normal discipline in Africa is abuse in the new country. In the strange land, you start from ground zero and work your way up. You consciously fight to retain your identity, to remain yourself, and, more importantly, to abide by God's principles. I remember when we got to the US, I was told to forget about my previous experience as an attorney and that the way forward in this country was to get a nursing degree. The fantasy life I had spun in my head of being a US-based attorney seemed decimated. I couldn't imagine being anything else but an attorney. Nursing was not even a thought. I had no passion for nursing, and I was not prepared to do something I was not passionate about. I spent days and maybe nights grieving over the seeming loss of the life I had. That was until I turned to God's word. I committed my life and my desires to Him. He picked me up from the place of despondency and gave me back what I thought I lost. Today I am a US-based attorney. Only by His grace.

And while you are working/walking your way up, your responsibilities to your parents, siblings, and community in Nigeria scream at you. Your phone never stops ringing. The requests for money and assistance pour in from all directions. There is so much to juggle. You are constantly trying to squeeze a dollar out of a nickel. You wonder if coming to America was worth it and begin to rethink your life. If this is not properly handled, parents could either pass on their frustrations to the kids or take it out on them. Either should not be an option.

Your children, on the other hand, are having the time of their life, making new friends, discovering new things, and in the process, becoming American before your very eyes. America is a very seductive society. The culture, mindset, and values consume your kids, but they sneak in on you.

Abram, unlike us, was on a journey to an unknown destination with God. He left his country, family, and everything he had always known at God's instruction. Abram was to follow God until God showed him his destination. Abraham lived in Canaan among a people that had no relationship with God. Despite Abraham's location, he kept the laws of his God. He was totally committed to the God who led him out of his country. What was God's blueprint for Abraham in this new country? In Gen 18:19, God said:

> *"For I have **known him**, in order that he may **command** his children and his household after him, that they **keep the way of the** Lord, to do **righteousness** and **justice,** that the Lord may **bring to Abraham what He has spoken to him."***

This is a very instructive passage of the Bible.

Several points to note from this scripture.

a. Known him: God knew Abraham. God vouched for Abraham. He was confident of what Abraham would do. He knew Abraham to be a person of integrity. That he kept his family on a leash. That Abraham was invested in the kingdom so much so that he would pass it on to his generation. Does God know and trust us as parents like he did Abraham? In a foreign land where others did not live by God's standards or worshipped him, Abraham stood out in his commitment to God. He did not change his commitment to God and his standards based on his new location. He took God with him everywhere he went.

b. Command—This is not politically correct in our generation. We are told to reason with our children, to let them make decisions, and not overreach. But God trusted Abraham to "command" his children. He was not to appease them, prod them, or give them a choice when it came to God's commandments. God could trust him to command them. They had no choice where God was concerned. No matter how we slice and dice the Word of God, it does not change his standard and requirements. God could trust Abraham to command his children and his household after him. This probably presupposes that Abraham would make sure His instructions were passed on. He was going to ensure that his lineage stayed true to God's commandments. They had to know that this was not open to discussions or debates. It was non-negotiable. It had to do with God, so it was sacrosanct.

c. Keep the way of the Lord: They were not to change God's instructions. They were to keep it. It had been passed on, and their responsibility was to keep it. They were not to debate its application for their day and time, not to tweak it to suit the exigencies of the day, but to keep it. The word of God is Yea, and Amen, so Abraham would command his children to keep it. To protect the word and keep it sacred.

d. Righteousness and Justice: God trusted Abraham to teach his children about spiritual, moral, and ethical issues. Amid a crooked and perverse generation, in a foreign land, in a cross-cultural world, Abraham's children were commanded to do righteousness and justice. They were to maintain God's standards and not shy away from justice. They were to obey God's precepts while championing issues of justice.

Standing against all forms of discrimination and inequity in the world.

e. God had made a promise to Abraham about his lineage: God had made Abraham a father of many nations. But the fulfillment of the promise was dependent on his children staying true to God's precept. Abraham needed to do this so his lineage could enter the fullness of God's promises and be great. Everything depended on Abraham commanding his children to stay in line. God gave him a promise knowing that Abraham would fulfill his part of the bargain. There was a generational blessing, success, and fulfillment connected to Abraham commanding his children to stick with God.

God is the same yesterday, today, and forever. His principles are eternal. A big part of raising successful children in a cross-cultural world is to COMMAND them to keep the way of the Lord. Knowing God and serving Him cannot be optional. We must do whatever it takes to get our children in line to preserve our generation.

Success, real success, is intergenerational. The blessing of the Lord must not stop with me.

In the United States, research shows that first-generation immigrants are less likely to be in the criminal justice system. They typically commit few, if any, crimes. However, as the generations become entrenched in the culture, they begin to show up in the justice system. By the fourth generation, there is no difference between them and American-born citizens. This is because we do very little to command the generation after us to follow the precepts of the Lord.

Parents must be intentional in setting an example for their children. As a parent, who am I at my core? What is my value system? How much of an example am I to my children? In Deuteronomy 6:7, Moses commanded the children of Israel to:

> *"teach them diligently to your children and shall talk of them when you sit in your house, when you walk by the way, when you lie down, and when you rise up."*

The word must be a lifestyle. Our children are inundated with the culture of the world at school, the television, the internet, billboards, and adverts at department stores. At home, they should be immersed in the word of God. Many children only hear the Word of God on Sundays at church. We must be intentional about teaching our children and living out the word.

We must be very vocal, intentional, and consistent about the values we want to transfer to our children. We cannot be lackadaisical about it. We must "annoy" them with it. Sing your values like a broken record. Our homes must be conducive places for the transmission of values. We must live and breathe what we preach. Children need to see your passion and not just mere words. Proverbs 22:7 says: *"Train up a child in the way he should go, and when he is old, he will not depart from it."* Training is intense. Some of our children are athletes who endure intense training, crazy hours, and sacrifice to get to the top of their game. It takes the same effort to train them in spiritual principles. We must be relentless in training our children. We should not just talk about the bible and our moral values. Train them, model it, be consistent, insistent, and unrelentless. Most children wake up early to catch the school bus on weekdays. We should be as intentional as we are about God as we are about their academics. Put God front and center of our lives and theirs. Children know if we are phony or fake. They need authenticity. We should not live a double life. We must live what we preach. God placed Children in families for a purpose; we cannot let them do anything they want to do. Even when it appears, they are not listening, it is being recorded in their subconscious, and at the right time, the word will become "flesh".

Which television shows do our children watch? What type of music do they listen to? Isaiah 1:18 says, *"Come now, and let us reason together"*, we should reason with our children about the importance of protecting their minds. Compliance with Deuteronomy 6:7 requires us to subscribe to channels that promote our value system. There are entertaining and wholesome Christian movies that we can watch with our children. We must win the battle for the souls of our children.

Africans are notoriously late. The concept of timing is often lost on us, but we must be deliberate about teaching our children about timing. Our children must be taught the value of being on time- to church, school, birthday parties and everywhere. We must model being on time and time management. Children need to understand the seasons of life and their responsibility at the different seasons. Ecclesiastes Chapter 3 says there is time for everything. Do not let them procrastinate. Use your vantage position to push them to do things even if they do not see immediate benefit. Be the adult and refuse to allow them to manipulate you. Make sure your child understands authority-spiritual and physical. It is not about unquestioned obedience to our culture but to the word of God. Our homes must be known for our adherence to God's command. God's word supersedes our cultures.

Wherever your "rivers of Babylon" is, God's commandments are non-negotiable.

# There We Sat Down and Wept

The children of Israel sat and wept in Babylon. These are two things that we must avoid. It takes nothing to sit down and weep, but it takes intentionality to make lemonade out of lemons. Weeping meant the Israelites' vision was clouded; they wept, and their eyes were shut to the opportunities that abounded in Babylon. They sat down and wept while others worked and made something out of their lives. There is always the temptation for immigrants to sit and weep because of dashed expectations in a new place or the indignity of starting from ground zero.

Nigeria's educational system is British and very different from the American system. My 6-year-old was in primary 3 when we left Nigeria, but American 6-year-olds were in first grade (the equivalent of primary 1). He had to go back two classes and be "behind" his Nigerian cousins. He was way ahead of all they were teaching first graders in America (I sat down and wept). After his first week of classes, the school had him tested for the gifted children's program, and he scored 55 out of 100 on one of the tests (sat down and wept). I was curious as to the questions he missed. I couldn't have anticipated what came next. The teacher told us he did not identify his surroundings accurately. He mistook the hallway for a corridor, the wardrobe for a closet, and the flashlight for a torchlight, amongst others. I was shocked. He got the answers correctly, and I protested. Well, welcome to American English 101, where we write the month before the day and the year. I sat down and wept when I realized my son had so much to unlearn.

I did not sit and weep for long though I got up quickly and did a deep dive into "Americanese". I researched all the free trainings available in my neighborhood. I took childcare certification at the YWCA, sign language classes at the American Society for the Deaf, and computer classes at the Jefferson County Library. It's okay to sit down and weep for a minute when you are overwhelmed with so much. But you need to get up knowing the destinies of your children are at stake. The focus must be on them. We live in a seductive world, and the seductions of the world are targeted at our children.

One of the many ways immigrant parents sit down is to get stuck in menial jobs. It is okay to start out small, but it is unacceptable to stay small. When we got here, I couldn't do anything because our paperwork took so long to process. I decided against any illegality, and so things were tough. I, therefore, opened an African store. I saw the store as a bird in hand, and I ran it with all my strength. Remember that I was a practicing lawyer in Nigeria, so running an African store was a step-down, but I knew it was for a season. That season lasted for six years (I wept and wept). As soon as it was possible for me to go to school, I started a master's program, passed the bar exam, and things began to look up for me. I started small, but I had my eyes on top. I later got a Ph.D., and today I am an Assistant Professor.

Sitting down in Babylon should be temporary. Our children need to see our example and aim high. It is not enough to tell our children what to do; we must be their role models. Too many immigrants get intimidated and refuse to improve themselves. I chose the classroom, and my husband chose the courtroom. He tells stories of fellow attorneys giving him an attitude when they hear his accent. They underestimate him, and that has won him some incredible cases. He refused to sit down though the environment was uncomfortable and unwelcoming. He has chosen to stay long enough to leave the door open for folks coming after him. Some are more focused on how much money they make in the short term and shortchange their future. It does not matter how long you have been on that seat. Get up and do something. Do something that makes your children proud. There is enough space for everyone to thrive. Get up and take your place.

There are very many reasons to weep in Babylon. The depravity of society vexes my righteous soul. Seeing how things work in Babylon compared with Zion can be painful. Coming face to face with your blackness and the attendant consequences is very jarring. Being treated like you are retarded just because of your accent – now that can be annoying. There are a thousand reasons to weep. But there is an African proverb that says, "When you are weeping, you can see". We must not lose our vision as we face these situations that sometimes make us weep. Our eyes must be wide open.

We must have our eyes wide open for opportunities available to black kids and guide our children in the direction of those opportunities. Being black isn't always a disadvantage. Being a Nigeria-American woman, I am intensely aware of the advantages and pressure that being female, and minority brings my way. The same goes for black men. Both parents need to befriend their children's teachers, join the parents' association, neighborhood association, and attend city council meetings. The Bible says, "My people perish for lack of knowledge (Hosea 4:6). Seek knowledge wherever it may be found. There are people whose lineage goes back 200-400 years; they have the knowledge we need. It is foolhardy not to associate with people in this culture. Seek them out and glean from them what you need. We need their knowledge to fast-track our journey.

One of the blessings of such an association came from one of my son's 6th-grade teachers. She introduced us to the Duke Talent Identification Program, which allowed him to take the ACT in the 7th grade. He scored a 26, and the program gave him a yearly $5,000 scholarship that paid for his summer programs from the 7th to 12th grade. They flew him to several university campuses for summer programs. Those programs were way out of our reach, but God positioned us in that school, and we availed ourselves of the relationship with the teacher. God always does his part, but we need to do what we need to do to get there.

We are citizens of Heaven living here on earth. Culture most times is contrary to God's plans and purposes for our lives. Every day, we make the choice to follow God and not the systems of this world. Everything tugs at us from different angles, and we are constantly asked to choose between "Jesus" and "Barabbas". We are products of culture and the culture we grew up in dictates our tastes, thought process, likes, dislikes, proclivities, and our world view. This is not to say that everything African is bad. Definitely not. Our cultural values include some biblical elements and precepts like generosity, honesty, respect for parents and elders, responsibility, and justice. Unfortunately, some of these values are not celebrated in society. Our goal must be to raise well-adjusted children and care for them physically, mentally, emotionally, spiritually, and financially.

The world's system tries to corrupt us and move us out of the domain of divine protection. However, parenting presents unique and sometimes frustrating challenges. Especially for African parents, the struggle is between three cultures-Godly, African, and Western culture. These are sometimes opposing cultures. While we can negotiate between the African and Western cultures, God demands absolute obedience. We cannot serve God and Mammon. As Moses told Pharoah, we must serve God with everything we have, and most certainly with our children. Unfortunately, most of our children are more in tune with Western culture than Godly culture. And more so, the enemy works hard to pollute the minds of our children while we journey to the promised land. Issues that arise while navigating these cultural issues can only be resolved by the grace, mercy, and wisdom of God.

# When We Remember Zion

My husband and I are lawyers. We earned our medals in Nigeria. We worked at a corporate law firm in Nigeria before we started our own practice in 1996. We were both up to something in the Nigerian society. Our friends were in positions of government, and I went back to school for a postgraduate diploma in maritime law to qualify me for judgeship in the federal court system. We were lining our ducks in a row, preparing for Kumbaya when we relocated to the United States. So, there was a lot to remember about "Zion". There was a lot to wish for. Many times, we smacked our lips remembering the normal sumptuous meals in "Zion", that became a delicacy in "Babylon".

It is natural to be nostalgic about the good old days. Remember, the Israelites remembered the cucumber and lettuce of Egypt and wanted to return to the land of their captivity. It is also tempting to remember Zion and live like a refugee in Babylon. Zion is the place of God's presence. It is the domain of divine protection. The children of Israel thought they could only serve God in Zion. They were blinded to opportunities to serve and worship God in Babylon, and so the remembrance of Zion brought tears to their eyes. They remembered Zion and wept. They thought their lives were over because they had left Zion. Things are different now. However, in a globalized, computerized, cybernetic world, there is no reason to remember Zion and weep. Take Zion with you to where you are. Zion is within reach. It is important for us 21st Century Christians to know that Zion is anywhere we are. We carry his presence, his glory, and anointing with us everywhere we go. The Israelites had no video recordings, mp4, 24-hour cable stations, internet, and all the conveniences we have today. They did not have direct flights to Zion, but we do. Rather than sit down and weep when we remember Zion, we can create Zion in Babylon.

Our children need to be taught about Zion. Many Africans regal their children with sad and sorry stories about their Zion. They do little to disprove Western media stories about Africa. They threaten to send their kids "back" to "Zion" when they misbehave. They tell them to finish their food because kids are hungry in "Zion". In one breath, you want your children to have an affinity for "Zion", and in another breath, you tell them how difficult life was in "Zion". You cannot approbate and reprobate. You need to label your trinket box accordingly. If you label your trinket box a trash can, folks will throw dirt in it regardless of how expensive it looks. Stop telling horrible stories about your Zion. Help your children have an appreciation of Zion. Give positive vibes when you remember Zion. Cry from nostalgia, and your children will hunger for Zion. There are important things you can do when we remember "Zion".

First, be proud of Zion. As the saying goes, "Remember from whence you were hewn". In talking about Nigeria, my husband frequently says there must be something good about a culture that has produced almost 200 million people, most of whom are doing well all over the world. There are good things in our culture. Celebrate them. Do not be focused on the things that aren't going well in Zion. Appreciate your culture. It takes light and darkness for plants to grow. Focus on a balanced picture of Zion. Do not elevate the American culture above the culture in Zion. The culture that produced you, gave you the values you have, and made you who you are, has a lot of good in it. Cherish and celebrate your culture, and your children will learn to love it.

Second, celebrate your culture. One of my friends set a day aside to celebrate her culture. In their home, when the kids were younger, Saturday was "Ibibio" day. Every communication is in the Ibibio language. They talk about family, call them, and do everything cultural on that day. Her kids were forced to learn the language because they could only get whatever they wanted if they spoke the language. The kids spoke with their grandparents, aunts, uncles, and friends in Nigeria on Saturdays. They ate their native food and watched Nigerian movies. This kept the kids close to their culture. I know this can be difficult if you are married to someone from a different culture, but it is doable. I know a couple who make this work. The wife is Japanese, and the husband is Nigerian. They speak both languages to the kids. The kids understand both Japanese and Yoruba because the parents speak their different languages to them. Research has shown that bilingual children are more likely to do well in school.

Third, share your vision. My father was a regular guy. He was very religious but did not have a personal relationship with God in the early days. But he understood affirmations before they became a thing. One of my earliest memories of my father was gathering us together to make some affirmations. It was in our language, Yoruba, but loosely translated thus:

"Momo pe Olorun loda mi"
I know God created me

"Momo pe Olorun kii seka"
I Know God is not wicked

"Momo pe ohun to wun Edumare"
I know God made me

"Lofi emi alara da"
Exactly the way he wants me to be

Nitori naa mi oni rahun lailai"

Therefore, I will never lack"

He made this affirmation for himself and enforced it in our home. My father understood the power of confessions. He understood the power of words. I can proudly say that I am a product of his affirmations.

The picture we set before our children determines who they become. In Genesis chapter 30, Jacob set a picture of stripped animals before the animals while they were mating. The timing and the importance of this is very important. He set the picture before them during conception and made sure they saw it. Literally speaking, the animals conceived what they saw. The timing and the picture were perfect. An African proverb says you can only bend a fish when it's fresh; any attempt to bend a dry fish will break it. We need to share our dreams with our children when they are young. The time to impart our values, beliefs, and culture is before they leave the house. The family is the first institution to which children are exposed. We must make good use of the first few years of our children's lives. Wake them up to pray. Pray for, and with them. Teach them the Bible. Let them memorize and recite Bible verses. Show videos of your home country and teach them the values, customs, and traditions you need them to know. It is almost too late when we send them out without equipping them with the tools they need to maintain their individuality in the world. When I was growing up in Nigeria, every home was like ours. The parents had the same value system. We went to school, and the teachers taught the same values and had the same expectations as our parents had; and if we misbehaved, any adult disciplined us the same way our parents would. Our parents' values were enacted all around us, so we had fewer reasons to deviate from the values and culture. However, the Western value system is antithetical to our values. Our values are described as prehistoric and antiquated. The school system, the neighborhood, and the laws in these countries demonize and invalidate the values in our homes. Our children are told they have a right to disobey our cultural laws, that they have a right to self-determination, they can choose their gender, and corporal punishment is abuse. They come home confused, sometimes angry, and discontented. Their reaction is natural. It is our responsibility to share our version of the "American dream" with them. Early, before the school, culture, and society get to them.

Full disclosure. I did a horrible job of handling these cross-cultural issues. I still remember when my son came from school one day and referred to me and his dad as "you guys". I hit the roof. That was very disrespectful to my African ears. I sternly warned him never to do that again. My husband was shocked but restrained. I wasn't having that. I remember telling my kids that everything American needed to stop at the door of my house, and they needed to remember that my house was the Nigerian embassy. Any time they told me something their friend was entitled to, and they lacked in our house, my response was the same "Do I look American to you". I was Africanly African. I wasn't having any of those things. I objected to the idea of being spoken to without reverence on every level.

There's so much I could have done differently. Thankfully we had a church community that helped "train" my children. They made up for what was lacking in me. Our home was decidedly Christian, and the church provided a platform for them not only to live their faith but also to serve God. We could have done a better job of helping them develop their faith, but we exposed them to people, activities, and programs that helped them develop their relationship with God. My son started playing the drums in church when he was 6, and my daughter sings in the choir.

In the average African family, parents are good at communicating their dream of academic excellence to the children, but we do a horrible job of communicating our values. We are better at enforcing rules than explaining the rationale for the rules. We do a bad job of listening to our children and including their ideas and comfort into our decisions. God's laws are sacrosanct, but he relates to us on the platform of love, which makes it easier to conform to his rules. We do not understand the modern expression of love. We assume that our children know we love them because we pay the rent, schools fees, and provide things they need. But as my daughter says, these children did not ask to be born. Provision is part of parental responsibility, and so we must not restrict the expression of love to provision. We must learn and practice ways to show our children that we appreciate them. The struggles our children go through are alien to us, but we can empathize even when we do not understand. It is wrong to minimize their feelings due to a lack of understanding. It is important that we acknowledge their feelings when we correct, instruct, and discipline them. When they do well in school, we must appreciate and celebrate. I didn't know it then, but this is probably why my daughter devised a means of being appreciated for making good grades. At the beginning of the semester, she would make a deal with her dad- she would promise to make all A's, and her dad, in return, will buy her a gift. To make sure the deal worked, she would print out a contract and make her father sign it. Needless to say, she always made all A's and got the pre-agreed gift.

This is probably un-African, but it works to schedule meetings biweekly, monthly, or whatever works for each family to check in and talk. Most offices have departmental meetings where we check in on projects and work through expectations. Our families should not be different. Aside from the regular prayer meetings/bible study times, we should have family time when we talk, share, and encourage each other.

# Carried Us Away into Captivity and Required from Us a Song

In Romans 8:28, the Bible says, "All things work together for good to them that love God, to them who are the called according to his purpose". The Israelites saw themselves as being carried away to captivity, and this informed their conduct and responses to their captors. How do you see yourself? What are you doing in Babylon? Ruth in the Bible is one of my favorite people. She lost everything in her country and followed her mother-in-law to a strange land. Her mother-in-law was very depressed, but Ruth trusted God to make a way for her. She did not allow herself to wallow in self-pity and despondency. She was proactive and went looking for work, believing that God would grant her favor. She understood the culture of her new environment and made it work for her. Her story changed because of her mindset. She became the grandmother of David, the man after God's heart, just by redefining and repositioning herself in a strange culture.

It does not matter how you got to Babylon. You must believe that ALL things work together for good. God brought you there for "such a time as this". Society needs to hear your voice; there is a song that God has put in your heart that the culture needs to hear. The story of Daniel is also very instructive. Nebuchadnezzar, a Babylonian King, conquered Israel and took some of the citizens captive. They were taken as refugees to Babylon, but as one of the lucky ones, Daniel was housed in the "White House". He was housed there because he had some qualities the King liked. He was gifted, talented, good-looking, and smart. He was taken into the palace because the king wanted people he could acculturate-it was something like the Green Card lottery that brought folks to the US. The boys were assigned someone to ensure that they understood, assimilated, and ultimately became Babylonians. It was an uncomfortable life to live. He missed his family and country for sure. But when life handed him a lemon, he made lemonade. He did not spend his time moaning about his condition. He adjusted to his new situation. He did not lose his identity as an Israelite, but he consciously did everything necessary to pick up skills and abilities and make friendships that made a living in Babylon easy. He learnt the language and culture of the Chaldeans. He assimilated into the culture. Daniel was cool with learning the language but refused to pollute his relationship with God. He chose not to eat food sacrificed to idols. He kept himself pure though he was far from home. A time came when the King had a dream that no one could interpret. Daniel prayed, and God gave him the interpretation. Interpreting the dream catapulted him to prominence in Babylon. Can you imagine how difficult it would have been for Daniel if he did not understand the culture, language, and food of the Chaldeans when he became the prime minister? I believe that some of our children have the interpretation to the dreams of this culture. There is something unique that only our children can do. Daniel "Sang the Lord's song in a strange land," and he won the heart of the King.

Change of location does not hinder God's plan for our lives. In Genesis 26:12-14, the Bible records that Isaac "began to prosper and continued prospering" in a foreign country. The children of Israel went to Egypt in search of food, and they became very prosperous in that land. Paul wrote most of the New Testament epistles from prison. His imprisonment did not negatively impact God's plan for his life. Esther started life disadvantaged, she lost both her parents and was adopted by her uncle. To worsen her situation, she was taken captive to Babylon. Her captivity activated God's plan for her life, and she thrived in Babylon. She did what other girls taken to the place did not do-she pleased the King's Eunuch. She chose not to despise the Eunuch, and God granted her favor before the Eunuch. She eventually became the Queen of Babylon and was instrumental to saving the entire Jewish race because she chose to sing the Lord's song in a strange land despite her captivity. So, whether you relocated in search of greener pastures, political asylum, educational advancement, sing. Sing the Lord's song. Do not let your circumstance determine your worship of Jehovah.

It does not matter if people see you through the prism of your captivity or your inadequacies. What matters is how you see yourself and your belief in God's plan and purpose for your life. We can and should thrive wherever we are. God always sets the table for us in the presence of our enemies. So, see it as an opportunity when you are required to sing the Lord's song. It is like God to showcase our love and commitment to him when we are required to do something at an inconvenient time. Anybody can serve God when things are going well. It takes a certain level of commitment to see and serve God in captivity. They do not have to require a song. Sing anyway, Sing.

# Mommy, Can I Change My Name?

In African culture, names are not just chosen because they are scintillating or trending. An Ibo proverb says, "when a person is given a name his gods accept it"- meaning that names are prophetic, they make a statement. They speak about the future of the child. They speak about the heritage, future, and the family the child is born into. In many parts of Africa, naming ceremonies are a big deal. It is not just a day of merriment, but a day when the family and community assents to the names given to the child. It is common for shouts of "Amen" to rend the air when the names are called.

Unfortunately, this understanding and attachment to names is not universal. I cringe when I go for doctor's appointment, and they do not make an effort to pronounce my name. My name is Omobolanle, and it means "a child that was born into wealth".

Funsho was 6 years old when he arrived in the United States. His full name is Oluwafunsho literally translated "God has given me to watch over". The name connotes that he is a precious child that God placed on his parents lap to carefully watch over. His parents call his name with pride. His name is a reminder of how precious he is. But that was until he arrived in the US. For some reason, they could not get his name right in school, and his name became "shawn", "fun", and many other variations. He endured it for a while and when he could bear it no longer, he asked his mother, "Mommy, can I change my name". He wanted an acceptable name like Shawn or Jeff, or Bill, something his teachers and classmates could pronounce. His mother was surprised but calmly asked him what Shawn, Bill, or Jeff meant and Funsho had no clue. She proudly explained the meaning of his name, and his face lit up. She told him many of the names he heard every day in school meant nothing and said nothing. She told him that every time his name is mentioned, it is confirmation that he is special to God and God had intentionally committed him to her parents to love, care and nurture. She encouraged Funsho to explain the meaning of his name to his teacher and friends. Funsho never asked to change his name again.

In Genesis Chapter 3, when Jacob had the encounter with the angel, it is instructive that the angel asked him, "What is your name?" Many have asked the question, what's in a name? The answer is a lot. For most immigrants, the name says a lot, in fact, everything. Let your children understand the importance of their names before society changes Oluwaseun to "Shawn", or Oluwakayode to "Kay".

Society has a different value system and different ways of doing stuff. Every immigrant family must take the time to have conversations at and around the dinner table often and consistently about their country of origin. Most immigrant children are inundated with the rhetoric of coming to America for a better life, escaping poverty, and/or coming to civilization. While that may be true in some cases, that is a "single" story. As Nigerian novelist Chimamanda Adichie points out, we are all in danger of telling or affirming a single story. We must tell the whole story. Our children need to know about the beauty of the traditional African society. They need to know the importance of the village in raising the child. We must buy books from the African Writers' Series and let out children know about their country of origin. There are tools that make this easier for us today. The internet has a lot of resources that can be used to drive this story home. There are documentaries online. There are movies from the African continent that show what life was like and the changes that have taken place in recent times. I am not unaware of the challenges of combining this with the hustle and bustle of life and the need to sometimes squeeze a dollar out of a nickel. But it's a worthwhile investment. Our children must not be mongrels; they must be well-versed in the culture and traditions of their countries of origin. It is dangerous for our kids to not understand our culture and why we think the way we do. If we do not pass these things on, we will live a life of regret in our old age. God himself was very intentional about the generations of the children of Israel preserving and passing on their knowledge of Jehovah and their values and culture to their children.

In Deuteronomy 6:7, God told Abraham to talk about them when he sits down, walks around, lay down, and all the time. It was important to ensure that the children understood the kingdom's tenets and that Abraham demonstrated the importance by how much attention he paid to it. The problem with many immigrants is that we drop the ball and just allow the seduction of this society to influence our children. Some even refrain from associating with fellow Africans in their bid to be more American than the American, and by the time the dividends show, it's usually too late to change course. I remember a lady who constantly told me in my early days in this country that she did not want to attend an "African" church but visited whenever there was a special program. I had no problem with her decision, but fast forward several years when her child started slipping in school and decided not to attend college. She then started running around and begging for us to speak with the child. She forgot that she had sowed the seed years earlier. Living in this country for so many years and watching those who made the wrong decisions in their early years have taught me that no matter how long you live in a foreign land, you are still an immigrant at your core. Your core values are almost always closely aligned with your "home" country. It is, therefore, important not to speak ill of your country. Love your country despite her imperfections. America, Britain, or whichever country you live in is not perfect. There is no perfect country on earth. It is, therefore, self-defeating behavior to not appreciate something about your country. Give a balanced picture of your country. Teach your children to love the country; after all, they love you despite your quacks. The Bible says the earth and everything in it belong to God. Your father owns the land. Make it yours redecorate it, get in the groove, and keep your head high -yes, you can

# How Shall We Sing the Lord's Song in a Strange Land

Alabama has a notorious history. It was the center of the civil rights movement, and people generally associate the state with racism, and so we often get asked, "What are you doing in Alabama?" One of our friends told us he would not live here even for a million bucks. But we have lived here for over 20 years, and the state has been good to us. We sing "Sweet Home Alabama" with gusto. And we love sweet tea with lemon! But it hasn't always been fun. We had a few bumps on the road., but we made a choice not to see Alabama as "strange" and to see the good in the land. The State opened up to us because we chose to sing the Lord's song despite the initial challenges of a new place. Singing the Lord's song in a strange land is a choice we must make despite our circumstances. I often compare our experience to the story of Jacob when he was running away from his brother Esau. He got to an unknown place where nothing seemed to work. It looked like His father's blessing didn't accomplish much. He needed to sleep, and all he had for a pillow was a rock. That was not a comfortable sleeping position, but Jacob used what was available. Despite his discomfort, he dreamt. That was us in 2002. Everything looked like the train left, and we were stranded at the station. But we chose to dream. Our heads were literally on a rock, but because we chose to dream, God brought our dreams to manifestation. I applied to almost every school when we got here, and the response was the same-I didn't have the requisite paperwork for admission. I tried to volunteer, but because I did not have a social security number for them to do a background check, no one would sign me up. It was incredibly frustrating, but I did not give up. I applied to the Alabama Bar to sit for the bar exam, but I got a rejection letter. Every door seemed locked against us, but we did not lose hope. Today, we are living our dream. Keep singing. Your song may not make sense now but keep on living. Someday, it will. Do not stop dreaming or singing because you are not in a familiar place. Your children need to hear and watch you sing the Lord's song. Singing the Lord's song inspires hope. It changes the atmosphere and repositions you for change.

We were intentional about keeping the memories of Zion fresh, so we made sure to call home regularly and get my kids to speak with their grandparents, aunties, uncles, and our friends though they had very few memories of them. It is also important not to forget your cultural diet. Most of the food from our countries are organic, they are healthier than the Westernized food we eat. It turns my tummy when I hear an African ignorantly and irritatingly say, "My kids do not eat African food". How did the kids decide what food to eat? So, long as there is no allergic reaction, kids should not decide what they eat. I had a timetable when my kids were younger. They drank "ogi" and "akara", beans and dodo, and everything African. They had no choice because I paid the bills. Children are not built to handle the choices that parents sometimes give. The Bible says, "Train up a child in the way he should go". You can "train" their taste buds, fashion sense, and social life. God never intended for kids to dictate to their parents; he expects parents to lovingly train, guide, protect, and instruct their kids. Our decisions may bring short-term discomfort, but our eyes must be on the long-term effect of our decisions. In Exodus Chapter 2, Moses' mother left him crying and ignored his tears. She was not distracted by her sons' tears. If she had responded to his tears and taken him home to soothe him, Moses could have been killed and missed his destiny. Her decision preserved him. Tears do not kill; let them cry. They'll thank you in future.

Moses grew up in Pharaoh's palace, but he understood God's covenant with the Israelites and internalized it so much so that he was willing to kill to ensure that the Israelites were preserved. The secret to his success was his mother, who trained him despite the overwhelming Egyptian influence. Moses might have turned out differently if the wrong person had cared for him. We must be careful in our choice of people to whom we entrust our children. There was something on his inside that resisted the comfort of Pharaoh's place and did not influence a change in his identity or perspective. The pleasures of Egypt did not overwhelm Moses. He was willing to forsake the pleasures because he was well taught. He was well prepared for life. God is the God of Abraham, Isaac, and Jacob. He is a generational and cross-cultural God. He reveals himself in the different cultures, and that is why he is the "I am that I am". Our children must know God as he is, and it is our responsibility to teach them.

# Understanding Your Child's Shape

Another tool to help in determining whether, how, where, and when to sing the Lord's song in a strange land is understanding who you are and knowing your child's SHAPE- The acronym shape stands for:

**Spiritual gifts:** The spiritual gifts your children have may not be manifest early in life. But we know they have gifts. A strange land is ideal to pray these gifts into manifestation or give them opportunities to manifest these gifts if we know what they are. It is important for us to model and emphasize godly character. Spiritual gifts without the requisite character can shipwreck anyone. We must deploy all our resources to monitoring, disciplining, and correcting our children so they can go out in the world to be like effective arrows in the hands of a mighty man.

**Heart**: What does your child love to do? I did not push my son to play the drums. He loves to play the drums. His heart beats differently when he is on the drums, and he has a covenant with God on the drums. I didn't know this early. I would hide the drumsticks from him when he was a toddler and yell at him to stop making noises on the drums. I am understandably biased, but I have not seen a better drummer anywhere in the world than my son. Watching him on the drums makes you worship God differently. The same goes for my daughter; she loves to sing. I pushed her to play the saxophone for a minute, but she found her passion for singing, and she is one of the best out there. Find out what makes your child tick.

**Ability:** This is probably the most obvious of the traits our kids possess. It is important to nurture this ability and give them the opportunity to train, retrain and develop whatever God-given ability our kids have. Do not look at your child's ability from a cultural perspective. My son loves to play soccer. He was so good in high school that some coaches were interested in recruiting him, but I refused to allow him to go to college on a sports scholarship. I feared he might get injured and lose the scholarship. Thankfully, he got an academic scholarship. However, he was so into soccer that he almost lost his scholarship because he was traveling with a club team playing soccer. I wish I had encouraged him to focus on soccer. I regret not allowing him to pursue his dream. Sports and academics are not mutually exclusive. If your child shows love for any extracurriculars, give the necessary encouragement and investment to help the child reach the highest potential.

**Personality:** Both my children are outgoing, but one is more sociable than the other. They are as different as they are alike. Comparing one kid with another is unwise. Every kid comes with the personality required to fulfill his/her potential. We must relate to them based on their personality type. Their personalities can be a pointer to their future and life goals. As parents, we must not try to turn them into people they were not created to be. I grew up with an extraordinarily smart but very reticent girl whose life goal was to be a teacher. Her parents pushed her to study engineering in college, and she struggled through her bachelor's. After her Bachelor's, she got a Master's and Ph.D. in education, and she is living her best life today as a teacher. Her parents chose a course for her which did not tie in with her personality. Thankfully, she found her voice early and made a detour.

**Experience:** The Bible says all things work together for good for those who love God and are called according to His purpose. I have found this to be true. Our life experiences as parents and even our children's life experiences can be a pointer to their future. The painful, not-so-painful, good, exciting, and exhilarating experiences may lead them to their destiny. Our children have experienced things that we know nothing about. Let's take the time to ask questions and seek an understanding of where they want to go, why, and how they want to get there. David's experience prepared him for Goliath. Paul's training prepared him for the ministry to the Gentiles. Peter's occupation prepared him to be the fisher of men. Luke paid particular attention to the miracles of Jesus because he was a doctor. What have your children experienced that is preparing them for the future? God may have prepared them at the backside of the desert. Ask, and they will tell you.

It is important for parents to know each of these about their children. Every child is different in their uniqueness. There's no one size that fits all. We must decipher what works for each child. My default mode is to prayerfully find out what God has put in each child. In First Corinthians Chapter 12, the Bible speaks about different abilities and gifts in each of us. Each parent should partner with their kids to discover what God downloaded in them. It makes parenting easier and informs the song and the tune each child sings in a strange land.

The example of David in 1 Samuel 17 is a case in point. Everyone saw Goliath as a giant. Trained soldiers freaked out and ran. The king was in sorrow over the threats of Goliath. But David knew he was anointed to take down the giant. He had the gift, the heart, the ability, the personality, and the experience to do just that. No one saw this in him, but he knew what he had seen God do when no one was looking, so he faced the challenge of Goliath squarely, and at 17, he brought deliverance to the nation. The King saw him as just a lad, his brothers saw him as a meddlesome interloper, and Goliath saw him as a dog, but David knew who he was, but more importantly, he knew what God could do from experience, so he faced the giant.

I wonder what David's parents would have done or said if they were on the battlefield. Would they have said No? You may be raising a David who looks nothing like it. I remember when my daughter told us she had joined the Air force ROTC. I initially took it as a joke, but when I realized she was serious, I asked several questions. I was shocked because I knew, in high school, she was almost always late to catch the bus at 6:45 am, and loved the good life. I didn't think she could endure the grueling training of the ROTC. I was also sure she couldn't wake up at 4:00 am to get ready for training. But I was wrong. She did all she was required to do and more. I didn't know my daughter like I thought I did. She is an Air force Officer and has won several awards that I would have thought unthinkable. Our children are growing up in spaces that pull out potentials locked up on their inside. Mary, the mother of Jesus probably did not know that she was breastfeeding the savior of the world and that the child she carried would soon deliver her. We need to see the invincible, so we do not become stumbling blocks in our children's path to greatness. If you train your children in the way they should go, they develop wings in the process, and you must trust that their wings work.

# Navigating Everyday Issues

Living in a foreign land is as exciting as it is stressful. Navigating everyday issues can make life especially stressful. Our children face these issues almost daily, and we should be equipped with ready answers to their never-ending questions. Some of these everyday issues include the following.

**Integrity:** This means doing what you say you will do when you say you will do it and how you said it will be done. Integrity encompasses the whole gamut of things, and our children must watch our lives and see the value of living right. We must keep our word to our children. If you make a promise, keep it. The concept of African time is antithetical to integrity. Our children need to understand the importance of being on time and getting things done when it must be done.

**Chores:** Children need structure; this teaches them responsibility. I am not sure why we think it is beneath our kids to do chores. In the early years, we had a timetable for food and chores. We cleaned and did yard work on Saturdays; My son cleaned the bathroom, and his sister swept and mopped the floors. They knew what they had to do, and I made sure it was done in sunshine or rain. Neither of them had fun doing it, but I insisted, and even today, when they come home, I still lean in to make sure they do not leave anywhere dirty when they leave.

**Bullying:** For some reason, kids do not think we will understand what they go through in school. My son, got bullied in school, but instead of telling us about it, he decided to take matters into his hands. He had enough one bright afternoon and beat and bloodied his bully. I was called to the school to pick my son at around noon, and I immediately called my husband, who got to the school as fast as he could. We were shocked at the facts we were confronted with. Our son was being suspended for 3 days because he beat and bloodied a schoolmate.

The back story was that the boy had bullied my son for weeks, and the teachers would do nothing about it. He was walking to class one afternoon when the boy and his friends took a swipe at him, but before they knew it, he took down the three boys and particularly gave the bully a broken nose. We were shocked because our son is low maintenance, stay-out-of-trouble kind of kid. Unfortunately, speaking with so many kids, I realized they assume we are tone-deaf to what goes on in their school. We must show empathy even when we can't relate with the facts of their situation. Get ahead of this, and discuss bullying with your child. Let them know you have their back and show understanding when they share things they endure in school. Don't minimize whatever bothers them. Show empathy and let them know you are there for them.

One major complaint I hear from immigrant children is that their parents do not understand them. This generation of children craves understanding. They need to know that they are not only seen but understood. There are also things that we say as parents that confirm this belief that we do not understand our children; for example, saying, "Why are you not like your brother?" or "Mrs A's daughter made all A's, why not you?".

Statements like this sting harder than we can imagine. Our children are sensitive. They are not wired like us, and their threshold for pain is thin. We must be careful not to pull down our children's self-esteem. We should correct and instruct constructively.

**Prom:** I am not pro-prom. I did not want my kids to attend prom, but they did. Not because I could not stop them but because I lost the argument against it. This conversation needs to happen before your child gets to the 12th grade. This is a very contentious issue between parents and their kids. The first person who told me about prom said it was a day when kids lose their virginity, so of course, I was opposed to the idea. However, one of the girls in the church told me she attended prom with her cousin. That works, I thought. I don't remember why, but they decided on a middle school prom when our son was going to high school. My first reaction was to tell him to pray and see if God wanted him at the prom. There was no way he would hear God because he was determined to attend, so I devised my own plan. I immediately volunteered to be on the planning committee so I could monitor him. I was shocked at many of the girl's alluring and captivating attire and makeup, but I stayed to make sure my son was not consumed by what I saw. Even if he were tempted or pressured into doing something untoward, knowing that I was a few feet away would make a difference. As busy as we are, we need to make out time to be a part of important, albeit social, milestones in our children's life. We must not assume that because bad things happen, they should not attend.

**Grades:** Every child is different. We must know the different abilities our kids have. Not all of them are good academically, but all of them can do well. It is important to know which child needs a little push or help and who needs to be left alone. And something that does not come naturally to a lot of parents is affirming our kids. We must go out of our way to affirm them and let them know that we believe in them. It means a lot when they know we are on their team. I do not compare my kids with other children, but knowing their potential, I push them to be who I know they can be. The problem is they do not see themselves as I see them, and at that time, I didn't have the vocabulary to communicate this to them, so it always came out like I was comparing them to other kids. Accept them for who they are-no comparisons. Our children must know that the best way to appreciate God is to show his glory in their academics. They must know that being content with a "C" when God endowed you with an "A" brain is unacceptable.

**Finances**: We taught our kids to give from an early age, but we did not teach them the whole gamut of financial principles. As a toddler, I taught my son that the Bible enjoins us to share because God gave us His only Son. So, whenever he refused to share his toys, I would ask him what does the Bible say?", and he would reply, "The Bible says we should share". Tithing is very important to us, and we drilled the principle into our children. I remember a time when rather than hand money over to us, one of our friends gave our son a large sum of money. We forgot to ask him for the money until a few days later. In his 8-year-old voice, he said, "Oh, that money uncle gave me? I gave it to God on Sunday". Our son had given the money we were banking on for the next few weeks in church. We pretended it was not a big deal, but a lesson learnt. They were already in college when we registered them for the Financial Peace University Course. It is very important to teach our kids financial principles. Teaching them to save is not enough". The tables turned for us, and it was my son teaching his dad about buying shares, what shares will do well in the future, and the different companies to buy from.

**Communication:** This is a giant elephant in the room of the parent/child relationship. I think I am a good communicator, and I know how to get people to do stuff. But communication has been challenging with my kids. They speak Latin, and I speak Greek, so it was almost always the third world war in our home. This generation is different, because I said so, does not cut it. We must painstakingly and nicely explain why we say so and why it must be done the way we want it, and when we want it. It is stressful, but it is the world we live in. We must know our children's language and make certain to speak that language when communicating with them.

**Visitors:** One of the tough issues in African homes is the presence of visitors. We had a three-bedroom house, so my daughter's room doubled as the visitor's room. It was never a problem (to my knowledge) because we explained to them how important visitors were and that they could stay for as long as they wanted. Though they both had this "my room" concept, I made it abundantly clear that they were my tenants. The rooms belonged to me, and I could do with it whatever I wanted; so, I shared the closet with my daughter. I am not an everyday kitchen person, so whenever I was in the kitchen, my daughter would ask, "Mommy, which guest is coming?"

My children got used to the constant pool of visitors, and it was never an issue. I had a friend whose mother-in-law came to visit, and after a couple of days, her 10-year-old daughter asked her grandmother how long she was staying because she needed her room back. The Mother-in-law was upset and blamed the parents for not training the child properly. We can avoid such embarrassment and bad blood if we have these conversations at the front end. Also, if your child's teenage friends are staying over at your place, make sure the same standards apply. Do not use uneven scales in your home. Be consistent in discipline and standards.

**Sleepover:** This was a sour topic in our home. My children didn't do sleepovers. I did not allow it, and I am sure they still hold it against me. But as I have told them both in private and in public, I have no apologies. I had read and heard a lot that happened to young girls and boys during sleepovers, so I avoided it like a plague. They never visited any of their school friends at home. My home was open to their friends, but they were not allowed to visit their friends. Do what works for you. The important thing is not to expose our children to danger. My children stayed over in the homes of my church friends, who I vetted and ensured had my value. That was it. I have read and heard so much about things that could go wrong at sleepovers, and I don't want to be included in the statistics.

**Friends**: My children claim (inaccurately, in my view) that I didn't let them socialize with their friends when they were younger. They had friends. And I recall dropping them off at several birthday parties at the skating ring, bowling alley, and parks. But for them, that was not enough. They wanted to have sleepovers with their friends, play at their homes and hang out after school. That was where I drew the line. I was okay with spending time with their friends so long as it was in public spaces. My daughter especially thinks that robbed her of valuable time to learn social skills and do age-appropriate stuff. I have no apologies. To her or anyone else. It would have been irresponsible of me to do different than I did. If I was wrong, I was sincerely wrong. And I still have no evidence that I was wrong. So, in the absence of any evidence to the contrary, I did right for my kids. Your situation may be different from mine. Evaluate your peculiar circumstance and make the best decision for you and your kids. Whatever you do, make sure you create opportunities for them to be kids.

In our bid to raise culturally aware children, we must not rob them of any of their any identities. This also goes for teaching our children about God. Our children must be trained enough to feel at home in any place where God is worshipped in Spirit and truth. One of the things I did with my kids was to expose them to a lot of people who parent like me. I am acutely aware that my parenting style is not common in their schoolfriends' circle, so I deliberately exposed them to other Africans so they can balance what they hear at school with their home life and know that I am different but not crazy. Part of singing the Lord's song in a strange land is realizing that the language of the Spirit is one. I may not worship or do things the way they are done here, but I am serving God all the same. I do not need to dumb it down to fit in. All I need is to seek avenues to educate people about how and why I do things differently. Our kids must take pride in their culture, food, and value. I was surprised but proud when my son wore Agbada to prom. I had no hand in that decision, but it is the offshoot of his pride in his culture. In our home, we ate African and American food, and never referred to clothes brought from Africa as African clothes or our food as African food. They are just clothes and food. My kids ate them, and though they didn't like them all, I had the privilege of hosting their friends and feeding them our food. I remember our son's first Thanksgiving in college, and he brought a Caucasian friend, to spend the holiday with us. I immediately offered my credit card for them to shop for food and whatever his friend needed. To my surprise, the two boys did not accept my card but told me they would eat whatever we cooked. His friend ate everything he was offered. Whenever my son played soccer for his club, his Caucasian friend carried the Nigerian flag. He is Nigerian by association.

We must respect our children in front of their friends. Do not put them down or scold them in front of their friends. Maintain your cool and affirm your child when there are friends around. If you must, please pull the child aside and do the needful outside the hearing of their friends. Also, if the children want to wear trendy things that we can afford, we should allow them as long as it is not against our faith and sense of decency. They must not be the odd one out every time. Looking good and decent helps their self-esteem.

## Health

The world has pushed the boundaries of aesthetics. People define themselves by how they look and what people say about them. It is important that we validate our kids daily and teach them to value principles and not just their looks. A lot goes into being healthy. We must promote all-round health-spiritual, physical, mental, and emotional- it is counterproductive to be spiritually healthy and physically sick. Our kids must do their yearly physicals and eat healthily. Children are less likely to enjoy healthy food and lifestyle, but it is our responsibility as parents to insist on all-round fitness. My children were involved in sports and recreational activities. They did karate, soccer, football, and volleyball and played drums and saxophone. They were never idle. It does not matter how busy you are; look for opportunities for them to be active. Some of these do not cost money either. Check the schedule in your local library, neighborhood activity centers, and churches. You will find activities that are either free or discounted. If your kids have the proclivity to be inactive, you may want to encourage them by participating in fun activities with them. Standards of beauty are constantly changing, and there is that pressure on our kids to subscribe to a standardized perception or look. We must affirm our kids. Tell them they are uniquely beautiful and encourage them not to lose themselves in the quest to conform to societal ever evolving and changing standards.

# Mommy, I am Pregnant.

I recently heard that one of the most anointed, popular, and contemporary pastors to come out of Nigeria was born to a single mother. To make matters worse, he does not know his father, and his mother died a few years ago. If his mother is still alive, I would have loved to hear her describe what it was like before, during, and after the pregnancy. I would love to know how her parents, the church, and her community responded to her pregnancy. I would love for her to share how hard it was dealing with the emotional, financial, and psychological stress of raising a boy on her own and in Nigeria.

Sometimes in spite of our best practices and efforts, life happens. It could be a teenage pregnancy, drugs, bad grades, or even a runaway child. I have had the privilege of walking alongside a mother whose unmarried son's girlfriend got pregnant and a mother whose daughter had a baby out of wedlock. Neither situation is ideal, but they happen to the best of us. Our children are responsible for the choices and decisions they make, and we must be okay with that. We have the responsibility to train them, but they have the right to do what seems good in their eyes. Our children are in a seductive society, and unfortunately, some fall into the seduction of the world.

Within the first year of our ministry, our unmarried church secretary got pregnant. I cannot discuss the range of emotions that went through me as the words "Aunty Bola, I am pregnant" filtered through my ears. She proceeded to apologize for disappointing me and said some other things I do not recall. I stood in the place of her mother, so I was understandably disappointed and angry at her. I wanted to scream and tell her how upset I was but could not form the words. I must admit that her attitude melted my heart and disarmed me. This lovely Christian girl made a mistake, and I resolved to protect and care for her. It was a journey, sometimes difficult and very challenging, but we made it. She had the baby, and today 27 years later, that "baby" is a college graduate, married, and doing well.

Being pregnant and unmarried is challenging. Coming from an African home makes it triply challenging. It's important as parents to realize that pregnancy out of wedlock is not the end of the world. It is important that our children know that we love them no matter what. Loving them does not mean we agree with their decisions, or we will not enforce boundaries; it means we are there for them for them if and when they need us. Our children need grace the most when they disappoint.

Don't get me wrong, your feelings of disappointment, anger, and embarrassment are justified. You have put in so much and done so much for this child who, in your opinion, has brought shame on the family. And it really gets under your skin if the child is not repentant and chooses to stay on the street. It is important to take a deep breath and see the God that makes a message out of our mess. He did it with the woman with the issue of blood. He ignored her history and validated her when others could not look past her dirty past. He did it with Sarah Jakes Roberts, the daughter of Bishop T.D Jakes, who got pregnant at 13 when her father was being touted as the "Black" Billy Graham. Her life took a downturn for several years, but God brought something beautiful, glorious, and exemplary out of her mess. She pastors a thriving church with her husband, and her mess has given her a platform that only someone with her past can stand on. Look past today's mistake and validate your child. We are not good at expressing our feelings, but please note that your child is not clairvoyant. Tell your child you are there until the wheels fall off. Be as supportive as you can. Your child needs you more than your money. We must protect our children from the judgmental people in our families. Create an environment where your child can share her feelings and you can help them think through the situation. If the child's father is in the picture, offer a hand of fellowship, and if there is a strain, do all you can to maintain peace. Remember that all things (including the pregnancy) work together for good, and the baby is not a mistake. God has a plan for the child.

# Hot Button Cross-Cultural Topics

The average African parent is lackadaisical about social issues. We naively think it is their problem and not ours. The problem is our children are growing up and confronting these issues, and, in some form, or the other, they must have an opinion and respond appropriately. We cannot afford to play the ostrich and avoid discussing these topics. Children are very impressionable, and we must write on the slate of their hearts before the school and society turn them away from God. I was very naïve as a young girl. Primarily because I grew up in a sheltered community but also because my parents told me very little about life. My father focused on our education, and my mother's primary concern was our moral chastity. So, all we heard were the dos and don'ts of girlhood. The world I grew up in no longer exists. Television, advertisements, the internet, teachers, and magazines at the checkout line all scramble for our children's hearts, heads, and attention. We must be proactive and fill their hearts with God's word and perspectives before they encounter the world. Information is everywhere, and first in time carries the day. It's a race against time, and our voices must be the first our children hear about life and societal issues. Our children must know where we were, and God took us to where we are. Our life experiences and our testimonies will make a difference in these conversations.

## Culture

God must be the center of our culture. The Christian culture is decidedly godly. There is no compromise. Our children must be immersed in God's worldview. Part of singing the Lord's song in a strange land is realizing that the language of the Spirit is one. I may not worship or do things like it is done here, but I am serving God all the same. I do not need to dumb it down to fit in. All I need is to seek avenues to educate people about how and why I do things differently. Make sure your child understands authority-spiritual and physical. It is not about unquestioned obedience to culture but to the word of God. Our homes must be known for our adherence to God's command. God's word supersedes our cultures.

## Dating

This is very controversial in Christian circles. You must set the rules you want for your children, and it is important to get their buy-in. I do not support dating for the sake of it. A good question to raise is purpose. Why do you want to date? Why can't you just be friends? Sometimes in answering these questions, the children will ultimately arrive at the right answer. Dating must be for the primary purpose of marriage. We must not date recklessly. We must date purposefully and after seeking the face of the Lord. Dating is not a sampling period. Jesus must be glorified in our lives.

## Inter-racial marriage

I have listened to African parents justify their disapproval of interracial marriage by referencing

Abraham's instruction to Eleazar to get a wife for Isaac from his kindred. Abraham's instruction to Eleazar was predicted on the idolatrous belief of the people in the neighborhood. It had nothing to do with race or ethnicity. He wanted Isaac to marry someone who had the same covenant with God. The Bible says there is neither Jew nor Gentile. Our attitude to cross-cultural relationships determines our child's willingness to open up to us at the nascent stage of the relationships. The children should know that you are open-minded and the goal is heaven. Our children should be encouraged to marry anyone so long as they are sure God sanctions the relationship. We live in a globalized world. The boundaries have broken down, and our kids mingle with children from different countries, and cultures. We must be open to our children marrying their soulmates regardless of their cultural or ethnic background. Racism should not be named among us.

## Same-sex Marriage

I knew nothing about homosexuality until my thirties, so you can imagine my surprise when my 13-year-old could discuss homosexuality. The school and friends got to my

child before I did. But for God! I was late in the game. As
sad as this sounds, quoting scriptures does not answer
the questions young people have about these issues.
Also, we must be careful to separate our disapproval of
homosexual behavior from our response to the
homosexual. Some children interpret our hatred for
homosexuality as homophobia. We must explain to our
children that God calls homosexuality a sin, and so must
we. The fact that homosexuality is acceptable in society
does not change God's word. God loves homosexuals but
hates homosexuality. Our children must be taught not to
apply democratic principles to God's precepts. We may
also need to reason with them about the behavior.
Telling my children that God created man and woman
like two pieces of a puzzle and anything outside of that is
unnatural helped explain this.


## Abortion

Abortion is being couched as a woman's right over her
body. We must be educated on the arguments for
abortion rights so we can intelligently answer our
children's questions about abortion. The overarching
question in this abortion debate is, when does life begin?

The Bible says God knew me before I existed in my mother's womb. As a mother, I tell them how I felt the first time I saw my children in the scan pictures. No one told me they were fetuses, and we could see and hear their heartbeats. So, killing a child in the womb is murder. In cases of abuse and incest, my belief is that those scenarios, as painful and disgusting as they are, do not invalidate God's plan for the child. We must painstakingly explain this to our children and patiently answer their questions. We must be careful not to focus on abortion and homosexuality as if they are the only sin.

## Racism

The lackadaisical attitude of African parents to the civil rights struggle and the challenge African Americans face confuses our kids. In the heat of the George Floyd crisis, one of my mentees told me about a conversation with her dad. Her father asked her if she had ever heard of a Nigerian being killed by the police? He concluded that African American confrontational attitude is to blame for the police killings. While in a few of the cases, this may be true, this was a rather insensitive response from this well-meaning dad. We must stand up for justice not just in words but indeed. God commanded Abraham to teach his children about justice, and so must we. Justice is part of our civic responsibility. When we fail to identify with the racism challenges our children face, it hinders communication in that section. Esther and Moses were not in the line of fire but understood the sufferings of others. Our children are first identified as black Americans before their name betrays their African descent.

## Politics

The people rejoice when the righteous rule. Politicians make decisions that affect our everyday lives, so the art of governance should not be left to ungodly men and women. We should encourage our children to participate in politics by voting and contesting for elections. No parent should discourage active participation in politics. The Bible says to occupy till he comes. Part of obeying this scripture is participating in politics.

## Pornography

This is an addiction that has eaten deep into the fabric of many a man. Pornography is all around us. It's on billboards, the front pages of magazines, and some of the movies we watch. We must be unequivocal about the dangers of porn. Do not bring just any movie into your home. Watch the reviews and discuss it with your kids. We must be aware that our children hang out with others who do not have our values. My advice will be not to pretend they do not know about these movies but to discuss it and make sure we are on the same page as far as values are concerned. I have a friend who watches trending movies with her kids and points out the issues in the process. Her perspective is that it is better to watch it with them than allow curiosity to drive them to watch it secretly with their friends. My advice is to prayerfully consider what works in your situation and let God lead you. Educate your children about how our five senses work. The senses are the gateway to our souls, and we must guard them jealously.

### Democracy

Democracy is a world system. It is not biblical, and neither is it the best form of government. Democracy has worked in some countries but is a colossal failure in others. Palestine, Lebanon, Egypt, and Iraq are examples of countries that voted terrorist and oppressive governments into office. God is not a Democrat. He is a Theocrat. And we must let our children know that the word of God is Yea and Amen and not subject to debate. The fact that homosexuality is acceptable in society does not change God's word. God loves homosexuals but hates homosexuality. Same for divorce, abortion, and all the other societal ills. Our children must be taught not to apply the democratic principles to God's precepts. Daniel had to make a choice between obeying the laws of God and the laws of the state.

## Appearance

Dressing: I am a stickler for professionalism. In Exodus 28:2, God instructed Moses to make clothes for Aaron and Hur for beauty and for glory. We must teach our children that the only cloth God designed for his priests are for glory and for beauty. That must be the standard for our clothing. Tamar was dressed in the attire of a harlot, and she was treated as one. James 2:2-3 speaks of a man dressed in "gay clothing" (nice attire) who was given attention and preferential treatment. What does your clothing say about you? As a parent, you need to stop paying for what does not align with your faith. I am not a fan of "distress jeans", low necklines, mini clothes, long slits, tight-fitting clothes, and a lot of the seemingly trendy clothes that our young people and, sadly, some adults wear today. The Bible enjoins us to be modest and dignified in our dressing. I believe in the "come as you are" but not the "stay the way you came" trend that we see today. I believe that Christians should glorify God in their dressing and that our clothes must be for beauty and for glory. I am aware that this thinking is in the minority. It is a battle. We win some, we lose some. As a parent, stand your ground but allow God to speak to these children. As my children get deeper into their walk with God, I have seen changes in their dressing.

## To Tattoo or Not

I am not dissing children with tattoos or their parents. This is an issue to discuss with your kids. There are divergent thoughts in the church on the issue, and tattoos are becoming mainstream. What do you know about it? Find out everything about tattoos and talk to your kids honestly about it. It is pointless to begin the conversation after the kids have made up their minds to have one. We must have that conversation with our kids about the undesirability of tattoos.

## Dreadlocks

This used to be taboo but is now mainstream. We need to discuss this with our kids. It is not enough to say it is unAfrican or unacceptable. Pick your battles and let your children know where you stand. It is true that dreadlocks may not take a child to hell, but will it take them to what will take them to hell? How does this impact their life? Does it bring them closer or take them further from their dream? We must reason with our children as they make this oftentimes life-altering decision. Remember, the Bible says all things are lawful, but **not** all things are expedient.

# Hannah or Peninnah

The book of Samuel Chapter 1, recounts the story of two women -Hannah and Peninnah- who were married to the same man. Peninnah had children, but Hannah was barren. Peninnah had sons and daughters and the ministry of provocation. Hannah's barrenness did not separate her from destiny, and Peninnah's fruitfulness did not position her for purpose. Children are a heritage of the Lord, but we must realize that it is not just enough to have children like Peninnah. Peninnah made a habit of going to the temple yearly and receiving gifts from her husband for each of her children. However, she did not make an eternal investment in the life of her children.

After Hannah got Samuel, she did something we must do as mothers. She chose to stay in the house and wean her child before taking him to the temple. She knew that her son had to be prepared for ministry at the temple. So, she took the time to wean him. She prepared him for his destiny. She weaned him well enough that when he got to the temple, he was not seduced by the ungodly lifestyle of Eli's sons. He was weaned enough that though the word of God was scarce, he could hear God when the prophet was deaf. He could see, even though Prophet Eli's eyes were becoming dim. He became God's man for the hour because he had a mother who weaned him.

Weaning is a very difficult, intense, and intentional process. It is not easy on the child being weaned. The child constantly kicks and screams through the weaning process, and no mother likes to see her child unhappy. The mother has to overlook the temporary pain and do what she has to do. Weaning a child is one of the tough decisions parents sometimes make. I am sure it was a hard decision for Moses' mother to leave her baby in the river. The Bible records that Moses cried in the basket. If she had taken him home because he cried, he would have been killed like the other children, and the plan of God for Israel would have been delayed. She ignored her son's cry, and like they say, the rest is history. While nursing him in the palace, she must have taught him about his history, heritage, and God's promises. It was her influence that ensured that Moses forsook the pleasures of Egypt and chose to suffer with the Israelites. Same for Samuel. He was everything God needed for him to be because he had a mother who made the investment at the front end to wean him before he started his ministry.

The choice before us is that of Hannah or Peninnah. We cannot be both. We must choose who we need to be in the lives of our children. The Bible says the wise man builds his house upon the rock. Jesus is the rock on which we must build our homes. The wind of contrary culture, entertainment, and storms are raging, but our homes will stand if they are built on solid rock, which is the word of God. Our worship must not be restricted to church services. Our homes must be Houses of Prayer where the Lord is honored and glorified.

Finally, as parents, the word must not depart from our mouths. Regardless of what our children do or fail to do, we must prophesy the word over their lives and create a future better than today for them. His word in our mouths is more powerful than anything the enemy may throw at them. At the end of the day, we win.

Made in the USA
Columbia, SC
06 July 2024

38129388R00063